Understanding Learning Difficulties in Mental and Autism Conditions

By
Ibrahim Gharibeh

Ibrahim Gharibeh

Copyright © 2025

Understanding Learning Difficulties in Mental and Autism Conditions

Dedication

To the heart that loved me unconditionally, my beloved mother, who left this world before seeing this book come to life, yet never stopped seeing the greatness within me.

You always said, "No one truly understands you, except me, only I know how deeply you care, and how much love you pour into your work for children with disabilities." And you were right.

Your belief in me was my first shelter. Your words were my first motivation. Your love was the foundation that carried me through every trial.

This book is more than pages and ink—it is a reflection of the values you planted in me: compassion, dedication, and the courage to keep going, even when the world doesn't understand.

Though you are not here to hold this book in your hands, I feel you beside me in every word, in every child I support, and in every silent moment of purpose.

I dedicate this work to you, with endless love and eternal gratitude.

Dr. Ibrahim Gharibeh
PhD in Special Education

Acknowledgment

I am deeply grateful to the children and families whose resilience and courage inspire my work, and to the dedicated educators, therapists, and caregivers who strive every day to make learning accessible for all.

I extend my sincere thanks to the AutizCare Foundation for its support in advocating for inclusive education.

This book is also a tribute to my late mother, whose unwavering belief in me and my work for children with disabilities continues to guide and inspire every step I take.

Dr. Ibrahim Gharibeh

PhD in Special Education

Understanding Learning Difficulties in Mental and Autism Conditions

Table of Contents

Dedication iii

Acknowledgment iv

Chapter 1 Introduction to Learning Difficulties 1

Chapter 2 Mental Health Conditions and Learning Difficulties 2

Chapter 3 Autism Spectrum Disorders and Learning Difficulties 3

Chapter 4 Assessment and Diagnosis of Learning Difficulties 4

Chapter 5 Strategies and Interventions for Supporting Learning 5

Chapter 6 Advocacy and Empowerment of Individuals with Learning Difficulties 6

Mental Health Trauma Procedure: Understanding and Addressing Psychological Trauma 12

Learning Difficulties Assessment Form 23

Learning Difficulties Evaluation Form 27

Author Biography 31

Chapter 1
Introduction to Learning Difficulties

Learning difficulties refer to challenges individuals face in acquiring knowledge and skills at the expected rate or in the typical way. These difficulties can manifest in various forms, including intellectual disabilities, specific learning disorders, mental health conditions, and autism spectrum disorders. Understanding the nature of learning difficulties is essential for providing appropriate support and intervention.

Chapter 2
Mental Health Conditions and Learning Difficulties

Mental health conditions can significantly impact an individual's ability to learn and perform academically. Conditions such as anxiety disorders, depression, ADHD, and bipolar disorder can affect concentration, memory, motivation, and overall cognitive functioning. Recognising the intersection between mental health and learning difficulties is crucial for implementing effective strategies and accommodations in educational settings.

Chapter 3
Autism Spectrum Disorders and Learning Difficulties

Autism spectrum disorders (ASD) are a group of neurodevelopmental conditions characterised by challenges in social communication, repetitive behaviours, and restricted interests. Individuals with ASD may also experience learning difficulties related to language development, sensory processing, executive functioning, and social skills. Understanding the unique learning profiles of individuals with ASD is key to fostering their academic success and overall well-being.

Chapter 4
Assessment and Diagnosis of Learning Difficulties

Accurate assessment and diagnosis are essential for identifying learning difficulties in individuals with mental health conditions and autism. Comprehensive evaluations—including cognitive assessments, academic testing, behavioural observations, and social-emotional assessments—can help determine the nature and scope of an individual's learning challenges. Collaborating with professionals from various disciplines, such as psychologists, educators, and therapists, ensures a holistic understanding of the individual's needs.

Chapter 5
Strategies and Interventions for Supporting Learning

Effective strategies and interventions play a vital role in supporting individuals with learning difficulties related to mental health conditions and autism. Personalised learning plans, educational accommodations, therapeutic interventions, and assistive technologies can help address specific challenges and enhance learning outcomes. Collaborating with parents, teachers, therapists, and other professionals can create a supportive environment that promotes the individual's academic and personal growth.

Chapter 6
Advocacy and Empowerment of Individuals with Learning Difficulties

Empowering individuals with learning difficulties related to mental health conditions and autism involves advocating for their rights, promoting self-advocacy skills, and fostering a culture of acceptance and inclusion. Educating communities, challenging stereotypes, and creating opportunities for individuals to showcase their strengths and abilities can empower them to overcome barriers and achieve their full potential. By working together, we can create a more inclusive and supportive society for all individuals, regardless of their learning challenges.

In conclusion, understanding learning difficulties in the context of mental health conditions and autism is essential for promoting equity, access, and success for all individuals. By recognising the diverse needs and strengths of individuals with learning difficulties, we can create a more inclusive and supportive environment that nurtures their talents and facilitates their growth. Let us continue to advocate for equal opportunities and empower individuals with learning difficulties to reach their goals and fulfil their potential.

Understanding Learning Difficulties in Mental and Autism Conditions

Addressing learning difficulties in individuals with mental and autism disorders requires a personalised approach tailored to their specific needs and challenges. Here are some strategies that can be helpful:

1. **Individualised Education Plan (IEP)**: Work with educators to develop an IEP that outlines specific learning goals, accommodations, and modifications tailored to the individual's needs.
2. **Multi-sensory Teaching Methods**: Use teaching methods that engage multiple senses to help with information processing and retention.
3. **Visual Aids**: Visual cues, schedules, and diagrams can help individuals with autism better understand and organise information.
4. **Sensory Breaks**: Allow for sensory breaks when needed to help regulate sensory input and promote focus.
5. **Structured Environment**: Create a structured and predictable learning environment to reduce anxiety and confusion.
6. **Social Skills Training**: Provide explicit instruction and practice opportunities to develop social skills and navigate social situations.
7. **Positive Reinforcement**: Use positive reinforcement techniques to encourage desired behaviours and learning outcomes.
8. **Collaboration and Communication**: Foster open communication and collaboration between teachers, parents, therapists, and caregivers to ensure consistency in support across settings.
9. **Emotional Regulation Support**: Teach strategies for emotional regulation and coping skills to manage anxiety or frustration.

10. **Professional Support**: Seek assistance from professionals such as special education teachers, therapists, or behavioural specialists to develop and implement effective interventions.

Remember that each individual is unique, and it's essential to continuously assess and adjust interventions based on their progress and needs. Patience, empathy, and a person-centred approach are key in supporting individuals with mental and autism disorders in their learning journey.

When assisting individuals with learning difficulties in mental and autism disorders, it is important to approach assignment completion with patience, understanding, and tailored support. Here are steps on how to effectively support individuals in completing assignments:

1. **Understanding Individual Needs:**
   - Take the time to understand the individual's specific learning difficulties, mental disorder, or autism spectrum disorder. This includes understanding their strengths, challenges, triggers, and preferred communication methods.

2. **Personalised Approach:**
   - Tailor assignments to cater to the individual's unique needs, capabilities, and interests. Consider breaking down tasks into smaller, manageable steps, using visual aids, or providing alternative forms of expression if needed.

3. **Clear Instructions:**
   - Provide clear and concise instructions for each assignment. Use simple language, visual aids, or verbal cues to ensure the individual comprehends the task at hand.

Understanding Learning Difficulties in Mental and Autism Conditions

4. **Visual Supports:**
   - Utilise visual supports such as charts, diagrams, or colour coding to enhance understanding and organisation. Visual aids can help individuals with autism spectrum disorder process information more effectively.

5. **Structured Routine:**
   - Establish a consistent routine for completing assignments. Structure the environment to minimise distractions, provide a designated workspace, and set clear expectations regarding deadlines and goals.

6. **Break Tasks into Smaller Steps:**
   - Break down assignments into smaller, manageable steps. Encourage the individual to focus on completing one task at a time to prevent feeling overwhelmed.

7. **Provide Positive Reinforcement:**
   - Acknowledge and praise the individual's efforts and progress. Positive reinforcement can help motivate and build confidence in their abilities.

8. **Sensory Considerations:**
   - Be mindful of sensory sensitivities that individuals with autism spectrum disorder may have. Create a comfortable and sensory-friendly workspace to support concentration and engagement.

9. **Encourage Self-Advocacy:**
   - Foster self-advocacy skills by encouraging the individual to voice their needs, preferences, and challenges. Teach self-regulation techniques and coping strategies to help manage stress and frustrations.

10. **Collaborate with Support Professionals:**
    - Work collaboratively with teachers, therapists, or support professionals involved in the individual's care. Seek guidance and input on best practices for supporting learning difficulties in mental and autism disorders.

By following these comprehensive steps and approaches, individuals with learning difficulties in mental and autism disorders can receive the necessary support and guidance to successfully complete assignments and reach their academic goals.

Mental health and autism spectrum disorders represent complex conditions that can significantly impact an individual's cognitive, emotional, and social functioning. Both mental health disorders and autism spectrum disorders are heterogeneous in nature, encompassing a wide range of symptoms and severity levels.

Mental health difficulties encompass a broad spectrum of conditions, including mood disorders, anxiety disorders, psychotic disorders, and personality disorders, among others. These conditions can manifest in various ways, such as emotional instability, irrational thoughts, behavioural disturbances, and impaired social interactions. Individuals with mental health difficulties may experience challenges in carrying out daily activities, maintaining relationships, and achieving their full potential in various aspects of life.

On the other hand, autism spectrum disorders are neurodevelopmental conditions characterised by challenges in social communication and interaction, as well as restricted and repetitive patterns of behaviour. Individuals with autism may face difficulties in understanding social cues, expressing themselves effectively, developing relationships, and engaging in activities that require flexibility and adaptability. The impact of autism can vary widely, with some individuals requiring significant support in multiple areas of functioning, while others may exhibit exceptional abilities in specific domains.

Understanding Learning Difficulties in Mental and Autism Conditions

It is crucial to acknowledge that mental health difficulties and autism spectrum disorders are not indicative of a lack of intelligence or potential. With appropriate interventions and support, individuals with these conditions can lead fulfilling and meaningful lives. Treatment approaches may include a combination of therapy, medication, behavioural interventions, social skills training, and educational support tailored to the individual's specific needs.

In conclusion, mental health difficulties and autism spectrum disorders are complex conditions that require a holistic and individualised approach to assessment, diagnosis, and intervention. By promoting awareness, understanding, and acceptance of these conditions, we can create a more inclusive and supportive environment that empowers individuals to thrive and reach their full potential.

Ibrahim Gharibeh

Mental Health Trauma Procedure: Understanding and Addressing Psychological Trauma

Introduction:

Mental health trauma is a serious condition that can have long-lasting effects on an individual's well-being and quality of life. Trauma can result from various experiences, such as abuse, accidents, natural disasters, or witnessing violence. In this detailed guide, we will explore the concept of trauma, its impact on mental health, and the procedures involved in addressing and treating psychological trauma effectively.

Understanding Psychological Trauma:

Psychological trauma refers to the emotional response to a distressing event that overwhelms an individual's ability to cope. Trauma can manifest in various forms, including post-traumatic stress disorder (PTSD), anxiety disorders, depression, and other mental health conditions. Common symptoms of trauma may include flashbacks, nightmares, hypervigilance, emotional numbing, and avoidance behaviours.

Effects of Trauma on Mental Health:

Trauma can have profound effects on an individual's mental health and overall well-being. Chronic exposure to traumatic events can lead to the development of mental health disorders, impacting one's relationships, work performance, and daily functioning. Without proper intervention and treatment, trauma can significantly impair an individual's quality of life and create long-term psychological distress.

Mental Health Trauma Procedure:

1. **Assessment and Diagnosis:**

    The first step in addressing mental health trauma is conducting a thorough assessment and diagnosis. Mental health professionals, such as psychologists or psychiatrists, use various assessment tools and diagnostic criteria to evaluate the nature and severity of the trauma experienced by the individual. This process helps in understanding the specific symptoms and challenges the individual is facing.

2. **Psychoeducation and Therapeutic Support:**

   Psychoeducation plays a crucial role in helping individuals understand the impact of trauma on their mental health. Providing information about trauma-related symptoms, coping strategies, and treatment options can empower individuals to take an active role in their recovery process. Therapeutic support, such as individual therapy, group therapy, or cognitive behavioural therapy (CBT), can help individuals process their emotions, develop coping skills, and work through traumatic experiences.

3. **Trauma-Focused Therapy:**

   Trauma-focused therapy is a specialised form of treatment that aims to address the underlying causes of trauma and help individuals heal from their past experiences. Therapeutic approaches like Eye Movement Desensitisation and Reprocessing (EMDR), trauma-focused CBT, or narrative therapy can be effective in reducing trauma-related symptoms and improving emotional well-being.

4. **Pharmacological Interventions:**

   In some cases, pharmacological interventions may be recommended to manage symptoms of trauma-related disorders, such as anxiety or depression. Psychotropic medications, such as antidepressants or anti-anxiety medications, can help alleviate symptoms and improve overall functioning. However, medication should always be prescribed and monitored by a qualified healthcare professional.

5. **Supportive Services and Community Resources:**

    In addition to therapy and medication, individuals with mental health trauma may benefit from accessing supportive services and community resources. Support groups, crisis hotlines, helplines, and advocacy organisations can provide emotional support, guidance, and practical assistance to individuals navigating trauma recovery.

Conclusion:

Addressing mental health trauma requires a comprehensive and multidimensional approach that considers the unique needs and experiences of each individual. By implementing a trauma-informed procedure that includes assessment, psychoeducation, therapy, pharmacological interventions, and community support, individuals can work towards healing, resilience, and improved mental well-being. Seeking professional help and building a supportive network are essential steps in the journey towards trauma recovery and mental health restoration.

Applied Behaviour Analysis (ABA) can be used to provide assistance to individuals with mental health challenges and learning difficulties. Here's a detailed step-by-step guide on how to incorporate ABA techniques:

1. **Assessment:**

    Begin by conducting a thorough assessment of the individual's specific mental health issues and learning difficulties. This can involve gathering information from caregivers, teachers, and mental health professionals.

2. **Set Clear Goals:**

    Based on the assessment, establish clear and measurable goals for the individual. These goals should focus on improving mental health symptoms, reducing problematic behaviours, and enhancing learning abilities.

Understanding Learning Difficulties in Mental and Autism Conditions

3. **Create Individualised Behaviour Plans:**

   Develop individualised behaviour plans that outline specific strategies to address the identified goals. These plans should incorporate evidence-based ABA techniques tailored to the person's unique needs.

4. **Implement Positive Reinforcement:**

   Utilise positive reinforcement to motivate and encourage desired behaviours. Positive reinforcers can include rewards such as praise, tokens, or preferred activities that are meaningful to the individual.

5. **Teach New Skills:**

   Use systematic teaching methods to help the individual acquire new skills and improve learning outcomes. Break down complex tasks into smaller, more manageable steps and provide ample opportunities for practice and reinforcement.

6. **Prompting and Prompt Fading:**

   Initially provide prompts or cues to help the individual perform desired behaviours. Over time, gradually fade out these prompts to promote independence and self-regulation.

7. **Data Collection and Analysis:**

   Monitor the individual's progress through ongoing data collection and analysis. Document behavioural responses, skill acquisition, and changes in mental health symptoms to evaluate the effectiveness of the intervention.

8. **Adjust Strategies as Needed:**

   Regularly review and adjust the behaviour plans based on the individual's progress and changing needs. Be flexible in modifying interventions to ensure continued growth and success.

9. **Collaborate with Other Professionals:**

    Foster collaboration with mental health professionals, educators, and other support providers involved in the individual's care. Coordinate efforts and share information to ensure a holistic approach to treatment.

10. **Monitor and Celebrate Progress:**

    Celebrate small victories and acknowledge the individual's efforts and achievements along the way. Maintain a positive and supportive environment to promote motivation and continued growth.

By following these steps and incorporating ABA principles into the intervention plan, you can effectively support individuals with mental health challenges and learning difficulties to improve their overall well-being and quality of life.

Mental wellbeing is a critical component of overall health and plays a significant role in our daily lives. It encompasses emotional, psychological, and social wellbeing and influences how we think, feel, and act. Maintaining good mental wellbeing is essential for coping with stress, fostering resilience, and enjoying a fulfilling life. In today's fast-paced and often stressful world, it's more important than ever to prioritise mental health and take proactive steps to support our emotional wellbeing.

One of the key aspects of mental wellbeing is self-awareness. Understanding our thoughts, feelings, and behaviours can help us identify patterns and triggers that may impact our mental health. Self-awareness allows us to recognise when we are feeling overwhelmed, anxious, or distressed, and empowers us to take steps to address these challenges effectively. Practices such as mindfulness, meditation, and journalling can enhance self-awareness and promote emotional resilience.

Maintaining strong social connections is another crucial factor in promoting mental wellbeing. Human beings are inherently social creatures, and engaging with others can provide comfort, support, and

Understanding Learning Difficulties in Mental and Autism Conditions

a sense of belonging. Building and nurturing positive relationships with family, friends, and community members can foster feelings of connectedness and reduce feelings of isolation and loneliness. Spending quality time with loved ones, participating in social activities, and seeking support from others during challenging times can strengthen social bonds and contribute to overall mental health.

Physical health and mental wellbeing are closely interconnected, with regular exercise playing a vital role in supporting both. Physical activity has been shown to release endorphins—chemicals in the brain that act as natural painkillers and mood elevators. Exercise can reduce feelings of stress and anxiety, improve cognitive function, and promote a sense of wellbeing. Whether it's going for a run, practising yoga, or taking a dance class, finding enjoyable ways to stay active can have a profound impact on mental health.

Cultivating a positive mindset and practising gratitude are powerful tools for enhancing mental wellbeing. Optimism and resilience can help us navigate life's challenges with greater ease and adaptability. By focusing on the good in our lives, practising self-compassion, and reframing negative thoughts, we can foster a more optimistic outlook and build emotional strength. Gratitude practices, such as keeping a gratitude journal or expressing thanks to others, can shift our perspective toward appreciation and abundance, leading to greater happiness and fulfilment.

Setting boundaries and prioritising self-care are essential for protecting mental wellbeing in a world filled with distractions and demands. Learning to say no, setting limits on work hours, and carving out time for relaxation and rejuvenation can prevent burnout and promote a healthier work-life balance. Engaging in activities that bring joy and pleasure, such as hobbies, creative pursuits, or spending time in nature, can recharge our mental batteries and reduce feelings of stress and overwhelm.

Seeking professional support when needed is a sign of strength and self-care. Therapy, counselling, and psychiatric services can provide valuable insights, coping strategies, and treatment options for managing mental health conditions. Talking openly about our feelings, experiences, and challenges with a trusted therapist or mental health professional can foster self-discovery, healing, and personal growth. It's important to remember that seeking help is not a sign of weakness but a courageous step toward prioritising mental health and wellbeing.

In conclusion, mental wellbeing is a multifaceted and dynamic aspect of our overall health that requires attention, care, and nurturing. By cultivating self-awareness, maintaining strong social connections, staying physically active, fostering a positive mindset, setting boundaries, prioritising self-care, and seeking professional support when needed, we can enhance our mental health and wellbeing. Investing in mental wellbeing is a lifelong journey that can lead to greater resilience, happiness, and fulfilment in all areas of our lives.

Understanding mental health involves considering a wide range of factors that can influence an individual's wellbeing. The interactions between social, cultural, biological, and personal influences play a crucial role in shaping a person's mental health. By exploring these influences in depth, we can gain a deeper understanding of the complexities involved in mental health and the ways in which different factors can intersect to impact an individual's mental wellbeing.

Social influences are an integral part of mental health, as human beings are social creatures who are deeply interconnected with their surroundings. The social environment in which an individual lives can have a significant impact on their mental health. Factors such as social support, relationships, and community ties play a crucial role in providing a sense of belonging and connection that can enhance mental wellbeing. On the other hand, social isolation, conflict, and discrimination can have detrimental effects on mental health, leading to feelings of loneliness, anxiety, and depression.

Social determinants of mental health, such as socioeconomic status, education, and employment, also play a crucial role in shaping mental wellbeing. Individuals from lower socioeconomic backgrounds or disadvantaged communities may face greater challenges in accessing

Understanding Learning Difficulties in Mental and Autism Conditions

mental health care, resources, and support systems, which can contribute to higher rates of mental health disorders. In contrast, individuals with stable employment, financial security, and access to education may have better mental health outcomes due to the protective factors associated with these social determinants.

Cultural influences are another important aspect of mental health, as cultural beliefs, values, norms, and practices can shape an individual's understanding of mental wellbeing and influence their help-seeking behaviours. Culture plays a significant role in shaping how mental health is perceived, stigmatised, and addressed within different communities. For example, some cultures may view mental health issues as a sign of weakness or spiritual imbalance, leading individuals to avoid seeking help or treatment for their symptoms. On the other hand, cultures that prioritise holistic wellness and interconnectedness may embrace a more integrated approach to mental health that includes spiritual, emotional, and physical aspects of wellbeing.

Biological influences are also essential to consider when examining mental health, as genetics, brain chemistry, and physiological factors can play a significant role in the development and maintenance of mental health disorders. Research has shown that certain genetic factors can increase an individual's susceptibility to mental health conditions such as depression, anxiety, bipolar disorder, and schizophrenia. Additionally, imbalances in neurotransmitters and hormones in the brain can contribute to the onset of mental health symptoms and disorders.

Moreover, biological factors such as chronic illness, traumatic brain injury, substance abuse, and neurological conditions can also impact an individual's mental health and increase their risk of developing mental health disorders. Understanding the biological underpinnings of mental health can help inform treatment approaches and interventions that target specific biological mechanisms underlying mental health conditions.

Personal influences are equally important in shaping an individual's mental health, as personal experiences, personality traits, coping strategies, and resilience play a significant role in how well a person can navigate life's challenges and stressors. Personal factors such as childhood experiences, trauma, adverse life events, and upbringing can significantly impact mental health outcomes later in life. For example, individuals who have experienced childhood trauma, abuse, or neglect may be at a higher risk of developing mental health disorders in adulthood due to the long-lasting effects of early adversity on brain development and emotional regulation.

Furthermore, personality traits such as resilience, optimism, self-esteem, and social support can act as protective factors that buffer against the negative impact of stress and adversity on mental health. Individuals who possess strong coping skills, emotional intelligence, and problem-solving abilities may have better outcomes in managing stress, anxiety, and depression compared to those who struggle with coping mechanisms and emotional regulation.

In conclusion, mental health is a complex and multifaceted phenomenon that is shaped by a wide range of social, cultural, biological, and personal influences. Understanding the interconnected nature of these influences is crucial for promoting mental wellbeing, preventing mental health disorders, and supporting long-term emotional resilience.

How to Break Bad Habits in Your Child

Breaking the habit of being yourself typically refers to the process of overcoming negative thought patterns, self-limiting beliefs, and unproductive behaviours that may be holding you back from personal growth and fulfilment. Here are some detailed steps you can take to break this habit:

1. **Self-Awareness**: The first step is becoming aware of your current thought patterns, behaviours, and beliefs that are not serving you well. Take time to reflect on your reactions, triggers, and habits that you want to change.

Understanding Learning Difficulties in Mental and Autism Conditions

2. **Identify the Root Cause**: Dig deeper to understand why you have developed these habits in the first place. Look for past experiences, traumas, or conditioning that may have contributed to these patterns. Understanding the root cause can help you address the problem effectively.

3. **Challenge Negative Thoughts**: Practise mindfulness to observe your thoughts without judgement. When negative or self-defeating thoughts arise, challenge them by asking yourself if they are based on reality or if there is an alternative, more constructive perspective.

4. **Create Positive Affirmations**: Replace negative self-talk with positive affirmations that support your growth and wellbeing. Repeat these affirmations daily to rewire your brain towards more empowering beliefs.

5. **Set Clear Goals**: Define the changes you want to make and set clear, achievable goals to work towards. Break down your goals into smaller steps to make progress manageable and measurable.

6. **Practise Self-Compassion**: Be kind to yourself throughout this journey of breaking old habits. Change takes time and effort, so be patient and understanding with yourself as you navigate the process.

7. **Seek Support**: Consider seeking support from a therapist, counsellor, support group, or trusted friends and family members. Having someone to talk to and provide guidance can make the journey of self-improvement easier and more effective.

8. **Engage in Self-Care**: Take care of your physical, emotional, and mental wellbeing by engaging in activities that nourish and rejuvenate you. This can include exercise, meditation, hobbies, spending time in nature, or any other form of self-care that resonates with you.

9. **Celebrate Small Wins**: Acknowledge and celebrate your progress, no matter how small. Recognising your achievements along the way can motivate you to continue breaking old habits and creating positive change in your life.

10. **Stay Consistent**: Breaking old habits and forming new ones takes time and commitment. Stay consistent in practising new thought patterns and behaviours, even when faced with setbacks or challenges. Remember that change is a process, and every step you take towards breaking the habit of being yourself is a step towards personal growth and transformation.

Understanding Learning Difficulties in Mental and Autism Conditions

Learning Difficulties Assessment Form

Student Name: _____

Date of Birth: _____

Age: _____

Date of Assessment: _____

Assessor Name & Role: _____

Section 1: Background Information

- **School / Educational Setting:**
  _____

- **Grade / Year Level:** _____

- **Primary Language:** _____

- **Relevant Medical or Developmental History:**

Previous Assessments / Diagnoses (if any):

Section 2: Areas of Concern

Please rate each area: 0 = No difficulty | 1 = Mild | 2 = Moderate | 3 = Severe

Ibrahim Gharibeh

Area	Rating (0–3)	Notes / Examples
Reading & Comprehension	___	_____
Writing & Spelling	___	_____
Mathematics & Problem Solving	___	_____
Attention & Concentration	___	_____
Memory & Recall	___	_____
Language Understanding (listening)	___	_____
Expressive Language (speaking)	___	_____
Social Interaction	___	_____
Emotional Regulation	___	_____
Motor Skills (fine & gross)	___	_____
Organization & Planning	___	_____

Understanding Learning Difficulties in Mental and Autism Conditions

Section 3: Learning Behaviors Observed

☐ Difficulty following instructions
☐ Requires frequent repetition
☐ Avoids reading or writing tasks
☐ Slow work pace compared to peers
☐ Easily distracted
☐ Difficulty transitioning between activities
☐ Shows frustration or anxiety during learning
☐ Strong reliance on visual aids
☐ Performs better with one-on-one support
☐ Other: _____

Section 4: Strengths

List the child's strengths or areas of interest:

_____
_____
_____
_____

Section 5: Recommendations

☐ Further diagnostic assessment (e.g., psychologist, speech therapist)
☐ Individualized Education Plan (IEP)
☐ Classroom accommodations
☐ Additional support services
☐ Parent training and guidance
Other:_____

Ibrahim Gharibeh

Assessor Name & Signature: _____
Date: _____

Understanding Learning Difficulties in Mental and Autism Conditions

Learning Difficulties Evaluation Form

Student Name: _____

Date of Birth: _____

Age: _____

Evaluator Name & Role: _____

Evaluation Date: _____

Evaluation Period Covered: From ___ / ___ / ___ to ___ / ___ / ___

Section 1: Purpose of Evaluation

☐ Initial evaluation
☐ Progress review
☐ End-of-program evaluation
☐ Other: _____

Section 2: Skill Areas Evaluated

Rate each area: 0 = No difficulty | 1 = Mild | 2 = Moderate | 3 = Severe | N/A = Not applicable

Area	Rating (0–3 or N/A)	Notes / Observations
Reading accuracy & comprehension	___	_____
Writing skills & spelling	___	_____

Ibrahim Gharibeh

Area	Rating (0–3 or N/A)	Notes / Observations
Mathematical reasoning & calculation	___	_____
Attention & focus	___	_____
Memory (short & long term)	___	_____
Listening comprehension	___	_____
Expressive language (spoken)	___	_____
Social skills & peer interaction	___	_____
Emotional regulation	___	_____
Fine motor skills	___	_____
Organization & task planning	___	_____

Understanding Learning Difficulties in Mental and Autism Conditions

Section 3: Observed Changes Since Last Evaluation

☐ Significant improvement
☐ Moderate improvement
☐ Slight improvement
☐ No change
☐ Decline

Details:

Section 4: Strengths Noted During Evaluation

Section 5: Challenges Still Present

Section 6: Recommendations

☐ Continue current support plan
☐ Adjust teaching strategies
☐ Increase one-on-one support
☐ Introduce assistive technology

☐ Refer to specialist (psychologist, speech therapist, occupational therapist)
Other: _____

Evaluator Signature: _____

Date: _____

Author Biography

Dr. Ibrahim Gharibeh

Founder of Autiz Mental Care, Dr. Gharibeh is a bilingual educational strategist, autism rehabilitation specialist, and internationally published author. His work bridges neuroscience, philosophy, and human empathy — challenging readers to see difference not as deficit, but as a doorway to deeper understanding.

With a literary and clinical voice, his writing translates complexity into clarity, and personal struggle into communal insight.

He speaks to professionals and families alike — shaping new conversations around identity, cognition, and perception.

www.ingramcontent.com/pod-product-compliance
Lightning Source LLC
Chambersburg PA
CBHW061226070526
44584CB00029B/4004